Introduction: A R... 5

The Articles of Confederation 9
   "Perpetual Union" 9
   Problems with the Articles 12
   The Call for a Federal Convention 13

The Federal Convention 15
   Washington Takes the Helm 17
   The Virginia Plan 18
   Wariness of the "Leveling Spirit" 23
   Crisis and Compromise 25
   Debates on Slavery 27
   Franklin's Speech 31
   "A Rising Sun" 34

Debate and Ratification 35
   Nine States 35
   George Clinton as "Cato" 39
   The Federalist Papers 40
   Federalists and Antifederalists 46
   Violence in Pennsylvania 49
   Ratification by Virginia 50

The Bill of Rights 53
   Jefferson on the Need for a Bill of Rights 53
   Hamilton's Opposition to a Bill of Rights 55
   The Magna Carta 56
   The English Bill of Rights 57
   The Virginia Bill of Rights 59
   The U.S. Bill of Rights 63

Epilogue: A Rebel Dies, a Charter Endures *by Wim Coleman* 65

Bibliography 68

In 1787, Massachusetts farmers, led by Daniel Shays, attacked the Springfield arsenal. (Library of Congress)

Introduction:
A Rebellion Sets the Stage

by Wim Coleman

In 1786, the United States had been independent from Great Britain for a decade. The Revolutionary War had ended in 1783, but all was not peaceful in the new nation. A new revolution seemed almost on the verge of eruption—and unlike the earlier revolution, this one threatened to destroy the Union rather than draw it together.

The poor and propertyless were suffering bitterly from a financial depression. In August, bands of farmers, desperate from debt and harsh taxes, started an armed insurrection in New England. They released debtors from jail and broke up courts in order to stop foreclosures and trials for debt. One of the leaders of this rebellion was a former officer in the Revolutionary War—Captain Daniel Shays.

In September, Shays and his followers closed down the state Supreme Court in Springfield, Massachusetts. Then in January, Shays led a small army in an attempt to take over the federal arsenal in Springfield. After engaging the rebels, General William Shepard wrote the following letter to the governor of Massachusetts.

Source: General William Shepard to Governor James Bowdoin, January 26, 1787; The Massachusetts Archives, 190, 317-320; in Longman's American History Online, http://longman.awl.com/history/home.htm.

The unhappy time is come in which we have been obliged to shed blood. Shays, who was at the head of about twelve hundred men, marched yesterday afternoon about four o'clock, towards the public buildings in battle array. He marched his men in an open column by platoons. I sent several times by one of my aides, and two other gentlemen, Captains Buffington and Woodbridge, to him to know what he was after, or what he wanted. His reply was, he wanted barracks, and barracks he would have and stores. The answer returned was he must purchase them dear, if he had them.

He still proceeded on his march until he approached within two hundred and fifty yards of the arsenal. He then made a halt. I immediately sent Major Lyman, one of my aides, and Capt. Buffington to inform him not to march his troops any nearer the arsenal on his peril, as I was stationed here by order of your Excellency and the Secretary at War, for the defence of the public property; in case he did I should surely fire on him and his men. A Mr. Wheeler, who appeared to be one of Shays' aides, met Mr. Lyman, after he had delivered my orders in the most peremptory manner, and made answer, that was all he wanted. Mr. Lyman returned with his answer.

Shays immediately put his troops in motion, and marched on rapidly near one hundred yards. I then ordered Major Stephens, who commanded the artillery, to fire upon them. He accordingly did. The two first shots he endeavored to overshoot them, in hopes they would have taken warning without firing among them, but it had no effect on them. Major Stephens then directed his shot through the center of his column. The fourth or fifth shot put their whole column into the utmost confusion. Shays made an attempt to display the column, but in vain. We had one howitz which was loaded with grapeshot, which when fired, gave them great uneasiness.

Had I been disposed to destroy them, I might have charged upon their rear and flanks with my infantry and the two field pieces, and could have killed the greater part of his whole army within twenty-five minutes. There was not a single musket fired on either side. I found three men dead on the spot, and one wounded, who is since dead. One of our artillery men by inattention was badly wounded. Three muskets were taken up with the dead, which were all deeply loaded.

I have received no reinforcement yet, and expect to be attacked this day by their whole force combined.

Shays and his men were soon repulsed from Springfield, and the rebellion came to an unsuccessful end in February. The leaders, including Shays, were tried and sentenced to death. But there was considerable public sympathy for the rebels and their cause, and Shays and his followers were pardoned. Moreover, many of their demands were soon enacted by law.

Nevertheless, the country was badly shaken. Could the new nation, so bitterly divided, last for long? Toward the beginning of the rebellion, George Washington expressed the anxieties of many of the elite and powerful throughout the United States.

Source: George Washington to David Humphreys, October 22, 1786; in American Memory/Library of Congress, George Washington Papers at the Library of Congress, 1741-1799, http://memory.loc.gov/ammem/gwhtml/gwhome.html.

But for God's sake tell me what is the cause of all these commotions: do they proceed from licentiousness, British influence disseminated by the tories, or real grievances which admit of redress? If the latter, why were they delayed 'till the public mind had become so much agitated? If the former why are not the powers of Government tried at once? It is as well to be without, as not to live under their exercise. Commotions of this sort, like snow-balls, gather strength as they roll, if there is no opposition in the way to divide and crumble them. Do write me fully, I beseech you, on these matters; not only with respect to facts, but as to opinions of their tendency and issue. I am mortified beyond expression that in the moment of our acknowledged independence we should by our conduct verify the predictions of our transatlantic foe, and render ourselves ridiculous and contemptible in the eyes of all Europe.

Not all influential Americans were so horrified by Shays' Rebellion. Thomas Jefferson made the following comment.

Source: Thomas Jefferson to James Madison, December 20, 1787; *The Life and Selected Writings of Thomas Jefferson*, ed. Adrienne Koch and William Peden, New York: The Modern Library, 1944, p. 440.

> The late rebellion in Massachusetts has given more alarm, than I think it should have done. Calculate that one rebellion in thirteen States in the course of eleven years, is but one for each State in a century and a half. No country should be so long without one.

But Jefferson had a fondness for rebellion that many of his peers did not share. For the most part, the insurrection provoked distress among America's most prominent citizens.

In May 1787, delegates from all of the American states except Rhode Island began to arrive in Philadelphia for a remarkable convention. Its purpose was to revise the Articles of Confederation, the constitution under which America was then governed. The delegates were among the most talented and knowledgeable men in the United States—"a delegation of demi-gods," remarked an awed Jefferson, who could not attend because he was in Paris.

To say that this gathering was summoned on account of Shays' Rebellion would be an exaggeration; the idea of such a convention had been raised from time to time for several years. But the Shays affair was much on the delegates' minds, and they spoke of it often and worriedly in their speeches and debates.

It is a curious irony that many of the Philadelphia delegates were fearful of insurrection, for that was exactly what they started during those four hot and quarrelsome months in the summer of 1787. In fact, the result of their work was nothing less than a second American Revolution, albeit a bloodless and reasonably orderly one. It took the form of the United States Constitution, to be followed by the Bill of Rights. Dwarfing Shays' Rebellion almost into oblivion, this new revolution transformed the identity and character of a new nation.

The Articles of Confederation

From 1781 until 1789, the thirteen United States were legally bound together by the Articles of Confederation—America's first real constitution. It was no minor document, but one which took a full five years to write, debate, revise, and ratify.

The nation was very differently defined under the Articles of Confederation than under today's Constitution. In fact, there was doubt as to whether the United States could properly be described as a *nation* at all, but rather as thirteen small and loosely-connected nations. In the minds of many influential men of the late 1780s, this very looseness was the source of countless difficulties—including Shays' Rebellion—which might ultimately lead to the end of the Union. The Articles, these men thought, needed to be revised.

"Perpetual Union"

The Articles of Confederation began with the following preamble and five articles.

Source: The Articles of Confederation, *Great Books of the Western World*, Vol. 43, ed. Robert Maynard Hutchins, Chicago: Encyclopedia Britannica, 1980, pp. 5-6.

Articles of Confederation and perpetual Union between the States of New Hampshire, Massachusetts Bay, Rhode Island and Providence Plantations, Connecticut, New York, New Jersey, Pennsylvania, Delaware, Maryland, Virginia, North Carolina, South Carolina, and Georgia.

Article One
The style of this Confederacy shall be "The United States of America."

Article Two

Each State retains its sovereignty, freedom, and independence, and every power, jurisdiction, and right, which is not by this Confederation expressly delegated to the United States in Congress assembled.

Article Three

The said States hereby severally enter into a firm league of friendship with each other, for their common defence, the security of their liberties, and their mutual and general welfare, binding themselves to assist each other against all force offered to, or attacks made upon them, or any of them, on account of religion, sovereignty, trade, or any other pretence whatever.

Article Four

The better to secure and perpetuate mutual friendship and intercourse among the people of the different States in this Union, the free inhabitants of each of these States, paupers, vagabonds, and fugitives from justice excepted, shall be entitled to all the privileges and immunities of free citizens in the several States, and the people of each State shall have free ingress and regress to and from any other State, and shall enjoy therein all the privileges of trade and commerce, subject to the same duties, impositions, and restrictions as the inhabitants thereof respectively, provided that such restrictions shall not extend so far as to prevent the removal of property imported into any State, to any other State of which the owner is an inhabitant; provided also, that no imposition, duties, or restriction shall be laid by any State, on the property of the United States, or either of them.

If any person guilty of or charged with treason, felony, or other high misdemeanor in any State, shall flee from justice, and be found in any of the United States, he shall, upon demand of the governor or executive power of the State from which he fled, be delivered up and removed to the State having jurisdiction of his offence.

Full faith and credit shall be given in each of these States to the records, acts, and judicial proceedings of the courts and magistrates of every other State.

Article Five

For the more convenient management of the general interests of the United States, delegates shall be annually appointed in such manner as the legislature of each State shall direct, to meet in Congress on the first Monday in November, in every year, with a power reserved to each State to recall its delegates, or any of them, at any time within the year, and to send others in their stead, for the remainder of the year.

No State shall be represented in Congress by less than two, nor by more than seven members; and no person shall be capable of being a delegate for more than three years in any term of six years, nor shall any person, being a delegate, be capable of holding any office under the United States for which he or another for his benefit receives any salary, fees, or emolument of any kind.

Each State shall maintain its own delegates in a meeting of the States, and while they act as members of the committee of the States.

In determining questions in the United States, in Congress assembled, each State shall have one vote.

Freedom of speech and debate in Congress shall not be impeached or questioned in any court or place out of Congress, and the members of Congress shall be protected in their persons from arrests and imprisonments, during the time of their going to or from, and attendance on, Congress, except for treason, felony, or breach of the peace.

Problems with the Articles

The Articles of Confederation went on to enumerate the powers of Congress—which, in principle, could declare war, make treaties, establish a national currency, and carry out other duties of a central government. But in practice, the Articles gave Congress little real power. The states remained sovereign and could obey or disobey Congress at will.

This situation led to considerable confusion in the former colonies. Some states printed their own paper money; some flagrantly disregarded the terms of the recent peace treaty with Great Britain. Congress could not collect taxes or build an army. Moreover, it was powerless to pay off the enormous debt incurred by America during the Revolutionary War. Such problems led to financial depression, which led in turn to outbreaks like Shays' Rebellion.

The banker Robert Morris, in charge of the new nation's finances, made the following despairing remarks in a letter to Benjamin Franklin.

Source: Robert Morris to Benjamin Franklin, January 11, 1783, *The Revolutionary Diplomatic Correspondence of the United States*, Francis Wharton, ed.; found in *The Declaration of Independence and the Constitution*, ed. Earl Latham, Massachusetts: D. C. Heath, 1976, p. 86.

Imagine the situation of a man who is to direct the finances of a country almost without revenue (for such you will perceive this to be) surrounded by creditors whose distresses, while they increase their clamors, render it more difficult to appease them; an army ready to disband or mutiny; a government whose sole authority consists in the power of framing recommendations.

The Call for a Federal Convention

In September 1786, delegates of five states met in Annapolis, Maryland to discuss commercial problems in the United States. The delegates came to a conclusion that was already being widely voiced throughout the country—that the Articles of Confederation were in desperate need of revision.

On September 14, the delegates sent a report to the legislatures of the states in attendance. This report was drafted by the brilliant young Alexander Hamilton, who would later become America's first secretary of the treasury. In the following passage, Hamilton voiced the convention's recommendation of a Federal Convention.

Source: The Annapolis Convention, September 14, 1786; in The University of Oklahoma Law Center, A Chronology of U.S. Historical Documents, http://www.law.ou.edu/hist/.

Under this impression, Your Commissioners, with the most respectful deference, beg leave to suggest their unanimous conviction that it may essentially tend to advance the interests of the union if the States, by whom they have been respectively delegated, would themselves concur, and use their endeavors to procure the concurrence of the other States, in the appointment of Commissioners, to meet at Philadelphia on the second Monday in May next, to take into consideration the situation of the United States, to devise such further provisions as shall appear to them necessary to render the constitution of the Federal Government adequate to the exigencies of the Union; and to report such an Act for that purpose to the United States in Congress assembled, as when agreed to, by them, and afterwards confirmed by the Legislatures of every State, will effectually provide for the same.

Though your Commissioners could not with propriety address these observations and sentiments to any but the States they have the honor to represent, they have nevertheless concluded from motives of respect, to transmit copies of the Report to the United States in Congress assembled, and to the executives of the other States.

Congress itself agreed with the conclusions of the Annapolis Convention and issued the following call for a Federal Convention. Note that in the language of this resolution, "the sole and express purpose" of the Federal Convention was to revise the Articles of Confederation. The delegates in Philadelphia were certainly not authorized to draft a new constitution.

Source: Journals of the Continental Congress, 1774-1789, Wednesday, February 21, 1787; in American Memory/Library of Congress, A Century of Lawmaking for a New Nation, 1774-1873, http://lcweb2.loc.gov/ammem/amlaw/lawhome.html.

Resolved that in the opinion of Congress it is expedient that on the second Monday in May next a Convention of delegates who shall have been appointed by the several States be held at Philadelphia for the sole and express purpose of revising the Articles of Confederation and reporting to Congress and the several legislatures such alterations and provisions therein as shall when agreed to in Congress and confirmed by the States render the federal Constitution adequate to the exigencies of Government and the preservation of the Union.

The Federal Convention

The Federal Convention was scheduled to begin on May 14, 1787 in Philadelphia's State House (also known as Independence Hall). But delegates from only two states—Pennsylvania and Virginia—were present. The state legislatures had chosen 74 delegates for the Convention, of whom only 55 attended. By the time the Convention ended in September, 42 delegates were still present; 39 actually signed the finished document.

A strict secrecy rule prevailed during the Convention; delegates were forbidden to discuss the proceedings with any outsiders, creating an atmosphere of mystery and intrigue. Moreover, suffocating weather added to the overall feeling of drama and desperation. Philadelphia summers are notoriously hot and humid, and those four months in 1787 were no exception.

The Philadelphia State House, also known as Independence Hall, where the Federal Convention met during the summer of 1787.

List of Delegates Attending the Federal Convention

NEW HAMPSHIRE
- John Langdon
- Nicholas Gilman

MASSACHUSETTS
- Elbridge Gerry
- Nathaniel Gorham
- Rufus King
- Caleb Strong

RHODE ISLAND
- No delegates appointed

CONNECTICUT
- William Samuel Johnson
- Roger Sherman
- Oliver Ellsworth

NEW YORK
- Robert Yates
- Alexander Hamilton
- John Lansing, Junior

NEW JERSEY
- David Brearley
- William Churchill Houston
- William Paterson
- William Livingston
- Jonathan Dayton

PENNSYLVANIA
- Thomas Mifflin
- Robert Morris
- George Clymer
- Jared Ingersoll
- Thomas Fitzsimons
- James Wilson
- Gouverneur Morris
- Benjamin Franklin

DELAWARE
- George Read
- Gunning Bedford, Junior

DELAWARE (cont.)
- John Dickinson
- Richard Bassett
- Jacob Broom

MARYLAND
- James McHenry
- Daniel of St. Thomas Jenifer
- Daniel Carroll
- John Francis Mercer
- Luther Martin

VIRGINIA
- George Washington
- Edmund Randolph
- John Blair
- James Madison, Junior
- George Mason
- George Wythe
- James McClurg

NORTH CAROLINA
- Alexander Martin
- William Richardson Davie
- Richard Dobbs Spaight
- William Blount
- Hugh Williamson

SOUTH CAROLINA
- John Rutledge
- Charles Pinckney
- Charles Cotesworth Pinckney
- Pierce Butler

GEORGIA
- William Few
- Abraham Baldwin
- William Pierce
- William Houstoun

Washington Takes the Helm

George Washington's diary entry of May 25, 1787, included the following typically laconic remarks.

Source: George Washington, May 25, 1787, *The Records of the Federal Convention of 1787*, ed. Max Farrand; in American Memory/Library of Congress, A Century of Lawmaking for a New Nation, 1774-1873, http://lcweb2.loc.gov/ammem/amlaw/lawhome.html.

Another delegate comes in from the State of New Jersey. Made a quorum. And seven States being now represented the body was organized and I was called to the Chair by a unanimous vote.

The choice of Washington as chairman was a natural one. As America's commanding general during the Revolutionary War, he was the nation's most honored hero. The records of the Federal Convention show that his role in the proceedings was almost entirely silent; he took no active role in any of the great debates. But it was said that a smile or a frown from him could sway matters one way or the other. If the following story has any truth to it, even Pennsylvania's redoubtable Gouverneur Morris found Washington a daunting and even intimidating presence.

Source: James Parton, Life of Thomas Jefferson, (1874); found in *Ibid.*

When the Convention to form a Constitution was sitting in Philadelphia in 1787, of which General Washington was president, he had stated evenings to receive the calls of his friends. At an interview between Hamilton, the Morrises,[1] and others, the former remarked that Washington was reserved and aristocratic even to his intimate friends, and allowed no

---

[1] i.e., Gouverneur Morris and the banker Robert Morris—also a Pennsylvania delegate, but no relation.

one to be familiar with him. Gouverneur Morris said that was a mere fancy, and he could be as familiar with Washington as with any of his other friends. Hamilton replied, "If you will, at the next reception evenings, gently slap him on the shoulder and say, 'My dear General, how happy I am to see you look so well!' a supper and wine shall be provided for you and a dozen of your friends." The challenge was accepted. On the evening appointed, a large number attended; and at an early hour Gouverneur Morris entered, bowed, shook hands, laid his left hand on Washington's shoulder, and said, "My dear General, I am very happy to see you look so well!" Washington withdrew his hand, stepped suddenly back, fixed his eye on Morris for several minutes with an angry frown, until the latter retreated abashed, and sought refuge in the crowd. The company looked on in silence. At the supper, which was provided by Hamilton, Morris said, "I have won the bet, but paid dearly for it, and nothing could induce me to repeat it."

The Virginia Plan

On May 29, Governor Edmund Randolph of Virginia presented the Convention with its first sweeping attempt at an agenda; this became known as the Virginia Plan. Even a hasty comparison of this plan with the opening paragraphs of the Articles of Confederation (see previous chapter) reveal a gaping difference. The Virginia Plan proposed a national government with three branches (legislative, executive, and judicial); a bicameral (two-house) legislature; and an executive consisting of a single person. This was a recipe for a powerful central government. If the delegates were to adopt the plan even in part, they would vastly exceed their legal authority, which was to do nothing more than amend the Articles of Confederation.

On June 15, New Jersey's William Paterson presented the Virginia Plan's only serious rival, the New Jersey Plan. This plan was voted down on June 19, and the delegates became increasingly committed to writing a new constitution based on the Virginia Plan.

Major William Jackson of South Carolina was elected secretary of the Convention. If the delegates had realized how sparse his notes would be, they doubtless would have made a better choice. For example, the following is Jackson's entire account of Randolph's controversial and vitally important presentation.

Source: Journal, Tuesday, May 29, *Ibid.*

Mr Randolph, one of the Deputies of Virginia, laid before the House, for their consideration, sundry propositions, in writing, concerning the american confederation, and the establishment of a national government

Fortunately for posterity, Virginia's James Madison kept a far more meticulous journal of the proceedings. In addition to being a remarkable note-taker, the future U.S. president was the Convention's most active and diligent delegate and has been called "the father of the Constitution." He has often been credited with essentially writing the Virginia Plan, taken below from his own notes.

Source: James Madison, Tuesday, May 29, *Ibid.*

Resolutions proposed by Mr Randolph in Convention.
May 29. 1787.

1. Resolved that the articles of Confederation ought to be so corrected & enlarged as to accomplish the objects proposed by their institution; namely. "common defence, security of liberty and general welfare."

2. Resd. therefore that the rights of suffrage in the National Legislature ought to be proportioned to the Quotas of contribution, or to the number of free inhabitants, as the one or the other rule may seem best in different cases.

3. Resd. that the National Legislature ought to consist of two branches.

4. Resd. that the members of the first branch of the National Legislature ought to be elected by the people of the several States every . . . for the term of . . . ; to be of the age of . . . years at least, to receive liberal stipends by which they may be compensated for the devotion of their time to public service; to be ineligible to any office established by a particular State, or under the authority of the United States, except those peculiarly belonging to the functions of the first branch, during the term of service, and for the space of . . . after its expiration; to be incapable of reelection for the space of . . . after the expiration of their term of service, and to be subject to recall.

5. Resold. that the members of the second branch of the National Legislature ought to be elected by those of the first, out of a proper number of persons nominated by the individual Legislatures, to be of the age of . . . years at least; to hold their offices for a term sufficient to ensure their independency, to receive liberal stipends, by which they may be compensated for the devotion of their time to public service; and to be ineligible to any office established by a particular State, or under the authority of the United States, except those peculiarly belonging to the functions of the second branch, during the term of service, and for the space of . . . after the expiration thereof.

6. Resolved that each branch ought to possess the right of originating Acts; that the National Legislature ought to be impowered to enjoy the Legislative Rights vested in Congress by the Confederation & moreover to legislate in all cases to which the separate States are incompetent, or in which the harmony of the United States may be interrupted by the exercise of individual Legislation; to negative all laws passed by the several States, contravening in the opinion

of the National Legislature the articles of Union; and to call forth the force of the Union agst. any member of the Union failing to fulfill its duty under the articles thereof.

7. Resd. that a National Executive be instituted; to be chosen by the National Legislature for the term of years, to receive punctually at stated times, a fixed compensation for the services rendered, in which no increase or diminution shall be made so as to affect the Magistracy, existing at the time of increase or diminution, and to be ineligible a second time; and that besides a general authority to execute the National laws, it ought to enjoy the Executive rights vested in Congress by the Confederation.

8. Resd. that the Executive and a convenient number of the National Judiciary, ought to compose a council of revision with authority to examine every act of the National Legislature before it shall operate, & every act of a particular Legislature before a Negative thereon shall be final; and that the dissent of the said Council shall amount to a rejection, unless the Act of the National Legislature be again passed, or that of a particular Legislature be again negatived by . . . of the members of each branch.

9. Resd. that a National Judiciary be established to consist of one or more supreme tribunals, and of inferior tribunals to be chosen by the National Legislature, to hold their offices during good behaviour; and to receive punctually at stated times fixed compensation for their services, in which no increase or diminution shall be made so as to affect the persons actually in office at the time of such increase or diminution. that the jurisdiction of the inferior tribunals shall be to hear & determine in the first instance, and of the supreme tribunal to hear and determine in the dernier[2]

---

[2] Last.

resort, all piracies & felonies on the high seas, captures from an enemy; cases in which foreigners or citizens of other States applying to such jurisdictions may be interested, or which respect the collection of the National revenue; impeachments of any National officers, and questions which may involve the national peace and harmony.

10. Resolvd. that provision ought to be made for the admission of States lawfully arising within the limits of the United States, whether from a voluntary junction of Government & Territory or otherwise, with the consent of a number of voices in the National legislature less than the whole.

11. Resd. that a Republican Government & the territory of each State, except in the instance of a voluntary junction of Government & territory, ought to be guaranteed by the United States to each State

12. Resd. that provision ought to be made for the continuance of Congress and their authorities and privileges, until a given day after the reform of the articles of Union shall be adopted, and for the completion of all their engagements.

13. Resd. that provision ought to be made for the amendment of the Articles of Union whensoever it shall seem necessary, and that the assent of the National Legislature ought not to be required thereto.

14. Resd. that the Legislative Executive & Judiciary powers within the several States ought to be bound by oath to support the articles of Union

15. Resd. that the amendments which shall be offered to the Confederation, by the Convention ought at a proper time, or times, after the approbation of Congress to be submitted to an assembly or assemblies of Representatives, recommended by the several Legislatures to be expressly chosen by the people, to consider & decide thereon.

Wariness of the "Leveling Spirit"

The records of the Federal Convention are surprisingly lacking in idealistic, ennobling talk about equality and democracy (neither word appears in the completed Constitution). Although the delegates were lovers of liberty, they were also, by and large, wary of too much democracy. With Shays' Rebellion still fresh in his memory, Massachusetts' Elbridge Gerry made the following remarks (taken from the James Madison's notes).

Source: James Madison, Thursday, May 31, *Ibid*.

Mr. Gerry. The evils we experience flow from the excess of democracy. The people do not want virtue; but are the dupes of pretended patriots. In Massts. it has been fully confirmed by experience that they are daily misled into the most baneful measures and opinions by the false reports circulated by designing men, and which no one on the spot can refute. One principal evil arises from the want of due provision for those employed in the administration of Governnt. It would seem to be a maxim of democracy to starve the public servants. He mentioned the popular clamour in Massts. for the reduction of salaries and the attack made on that of the Govr. though secured by the spirit of the Constitution itself. He had he said been too republican heretofore: he was still however republican, but had been taught by experience the danger of the levilling spirit.

Some delegates, like Delaware's John Dickinson, expressed a frank preference for some kind of monarchy, even while admitting its impossibility in America (taken from Madison's notes).

Source: James Madison, Saturday, June 2, *Ibid*.

A limited Monarchy [Dickinson] considered as one of the best Governments in the world. It was not certain that the same blessings were derivable from any other form. It was certain that equal blessings had never yet been derived from any of the republican form. A limited monarchy however was out of the question. The spirit of the times—the state of our affairs, forbade the experiment, if it were desireable. Was it possible moreover in the nature of things to introduce it even if these obstacles were less insuperable. A House of Nobles was essential to such a Govt. Could these be created by a breath, or by a stroke of the pen? No. They were the growth of ages, and could only arise under a complication of circumstances none of which existed in this Country. But though a form the most perfect perhaps in itself be unattainable, we must not despair. If antient republics have been found to flourish for a moment only & then vanish forever, it only proves that they were badly constituted; and that we ought to seek for every remedy for their diseases.

In his unsuccessful bid to interest the Convention in his own plan for a constitution, Alexander Hamilton reserved his harshest words for democracy (taken from the notes of New York's Robert Yates).

The voice of the people has been said to be the voice of God; and however generally this maxim has been quoted and believed, it is not true in fact. The people are turbulent and changing; they seldom judge or determine right. Give therefore to the first class a distinct, permanent share in the government. They will check the unsteadiness of the second, and as they cannot receive any advantage by a change, they therefore will ever maintain good government. Can a democratic assembly, who annually revolve in the mass of the people, be supposed steadily to pursue the public good? Nothing but a permanent body can check the imprudence of democracy. Their turbulent and uncontrouling disposition requires checks.

Crisis and Compromise

Most elements of the Virginia Plan were accepted by the Convention. Nevertheless, delegates from smaller states were alarmed by the plan's insistence on proportional representation in both legislatures. This meant that small states would have fewer representatives. For a solid month, the small and large states were deadlocked on this issue, and the Convention itself seemed on the verge of breaking up. On June 10, George Washington wrote this despairing letter to Alexander Hamilton, who had left the Convention on June 30 when his own ideas attracted no support.

Source: George Washington to Alexander Hamilton, July 10, 1787; *Ibid.*

I thank you for your communication of the 3d.—When I refer you to the state of the Councils which prevailed at the period you left this City—and add, that they are now, if possible, in a worse train than ever; you will find but little ground on which the hope of a good establishment can be formed.—In a word, I almost despair of seeing a favourable issue to the proceedings of the Convention, and do therefore repent having had any agency in the business.

The Men who oppose a strong & energetic government are, in my opinion, narrow minded politicians, or are under the influence of local views. The apprehension expressed by them that the people will not accede to the form proposed is the ostensible, not the real cause of the opposition but admitting that the present sentiment is as they prognosticate, the question ought nevertheless to be, is it, or is it not, the best form?—If the former, recommend it, and it will assuredly obtain mauger opposition

I am sorry you went away—I wish you were back.—The crisis is equally important and alarming, and no opposition under such circumstances should discourage exertions till the signature is fixed.—I will not, at this time trouble you with more than my best wishes and sincere regards.

On July 16, the deadlock was broken. The first branch of the legislature (which would become the House of Representatives) was, indeed, to be proportional in representation. But the second branch (which would become the Senate) was to be equal in representation. Delegates from smaller states were delighted; those from the larger states were bitter. But their bitterness was futile, as James Madison noted in his journal.

Source: James Madison, Monday, July 16, *Ibid*.

On the morning following before the hour of the Convention a number of the members from the larger States, by common agreement met for the purpose of consulting on the proper steps to be taken in consequence of the vote in favor of an equal Representation in the 2d. branch, and the apparent inflexibility of the smaller States on that point— Several members from the latter States also attended. The time was wasted in vague conversation on the subject, without any specific proposition or agreement.

Debates on Slavery

On Monday, August 6, the Committee of Detail (consisting of Virginia's Edmund Randolph, Pennsylvania's James Wilson, South Carolina's John Rutledge, Massachusetts' Nathaniel Gorham, and Connecticut's Oliver Ellsworth) presented a report on the Convention's work so far. Much had been resolved, but much remained unresolved—including how to deal with the grim issue of slavery.

Southern delegates were anxious that the national government not try to limit or end slave imports. They also wanted slaves partially counted as population for the purpose of determining taxation and legislative representation; five slaves were to be equal to three free whites. Madison's notes related Gouverneur Morris' furious response to this concept (which actually became part of the Constitution).

Source: James Madison, Wednesday, August 8, *Ibid.*

[Gouverneur Morris] never would concur in upholding domestic slavery. It was a nefarious institution—It was the curse of heaven on the States where it prevailed. Compare the free regions of the Middle States, where a rich & noble cultivation marks the prosperity & happiness of the people, with the misery & poverty which overspread the barren wastes of Va. Maryd. & the other States having slaves. Travel thro' ye whole Continent & you behold the prospect continually varying with the appearance & disappearance of slavery. The moment you leave ye E. Sts. & enter N. York, the effects of the institution become visible; Passing thro' the Jerseys and entering every criterion of superior improvement witnesses the change. Proceed Southwdly, & every step you take thro' ye great regions of slaves, presents a desert increasing with ye increasing proportion of these wretched beings.

Upon what principle is it that the slaves shall be computed in the representation? Are they men? Then make them

Citizens & let them vote? Are they property? Why then is no other property included? The Houses in this City (Philada.) are worth more than all the wretched slaves which cover the rice swamps of South Carolina. The admission of slaves into the Representation when fairly explained comes to this: that the inhabitant of Georgia and S. C. who goes to the Coast of Africa, and in defiance of the most sacred laws of humanity tears away his fellow creatures from their dearest connections & dam(n)s them to the most cruel bondages, shall have more votes in a Govt. instituted for protection of the rights of mankind, than the Citizen of Pa or N. Jersey who views with a laudable horror, so nefarious a practice. He would add that Domestic slavery is the most prominent feature in the aristocratic countenance of the proposed Constitution. The vassalage of the poor has ever been the favorite offspring of Aristocracy. And What is the proposed compensation to the Northern States for a sacrifice of every principle of right, of every impulse of humanity. They are to bind themselves to march their militia for the defence of the S. States; for their defence agst those very slaves of whom they complain. They must supply vessels & seamen, in case of foreign Attack. The Legislature will have indefinite power to tax them by excises, and duties on imports: both of which will fall heavier on them than on the Southern inhabitants; for the bohea tea[3] used by a Northern freeman, will pay more tax than the whole consumption of the miserable slave, which consists of nothing more than his physical subsistence and the rag that covers his nakedness. On the other side the Southern States are not to be restrained from importing fresh supplies of wretched Africans, at once to increase the danger of

---

[3] Black tea.

attack, and the difficulty of defence; nay they are to be encouraged to it by an assurance of having their votes in the Natl Govt increased in proportion. and are at the same time to have their exports & their slaves exempt from all contributions for the public service. Let it not be said that direct taxation is to be proportioned to representation. It is idle to suppose that the Genl Govt. can stretch its hand directly into the pockets of the people scattered over so vast a Country. They can only do it through the medium of exports imports & excises. For what then are all these sacrifices to be made? He would sooner submit himself to a tax for paying for all the Negroes in the U. States. than saddle posterity with such a Constitution.

As the debate continued during the days that followed, John Rutledge of South Carolina coolly argued in favor of counting slaves as population.

Source: James Madison, Tuesday, August 21, *Ibid.*

Mr Rutlidge did not see how the importation of slaves could be encouraged by this section. He was not apprehensive of insurrections and would readily exempt the other States from (the obligation to protect the Southern against them.). — Religion & humanity had nothing to do with this question — Interest alone is the governing principle with Nations — The true question at present is whether the Southn. States shall or shall not be parties to the Union. If the Northern States consult their interest, they will not oppose the increase of Slaves which will increase the commodities of which they will become the carriers.

When the possibility was raised of granting the national government the power to end slave importation, young Charles Pinckney of South Carolina vigorously argued against it; he even endeavored to defend moral rightness of slavery.

Source: James Madison, Wednesday, August 22, *Ibid.*

Mr. Pinkney — If slavery be wrong, it is justified by the example of all the world. He cited the case of Greece Rome & other antient States; the sanction given by France England, Holland & other modern States. In all ages one half of mankind have been slaves. If the S. States were let alone they will probably of themselves stop importations. He wd. himself as a Citizen of S. Carolina vote for it. An attempt to take away the right as proposed will produce serious objections to the Constitution which he wished to see adopted.

Delaware's John Dickinson made the following response to Pinckney's remarks. (Ultimately, the delegates agreed that the Constitution would allow the importation of slaves until 1808.)

Source: *Ibid.*

Mr. Dickenson considered it as inadmissible on every principle of honor & safety that the importation of slaves should be authorized to the States by the Constitution. The true question was whether the national happiness would be promoted or impeded by the importation, and this question ought to be left to the National Govt. not to the States particularly interested. If Engd. & France permit slavery, slaves are at the same time excluded from both those Kingdoms. Greece and Rome were made unhappy by their slaves. He could not believe that the Southn. States would refuse to confederate on the account apprehended; especially as the power was not likely to be immediately exercised by the Genl. Government.

Franklin's Speech

Five more weeks of suffocating weather and often rancorous debate passed after the Committee of Detail gave its report. On September 12, the Committee of Style (consisting of Connecticut's William Samuel Johnson, Massachusetts' Rufus King, Gouverneur Morris, James Madison, and Alexander Hamilton, who had returned to the Convention) presented a draft of the Constitution itself. Gouverneur Morris' graceful prose was evident throughout the document, especially in its preamble.

The remaining debate was swift and brutal. But on September 15, the Convention approved the Constitution, despite probable misgivings on the part of every delegate present.

At 82 years of age, Benjamin Franklin was by far the oldest delegate at the convention—and along with Washington, the most deeply respected. But also like Washington, Franklin's actual contributions to the Constitution were surprisingly few. Franklin's failed ideas included a one-house legislature, an executive of more than one person, and unsalaried officials.

But Franklin's very presence at the convention was valuable—perhaps even crucial. His most important moment came on the morning of September 17, just before the Constitution was to be signed by the delegates. Too ill and feeble to speak at length himself, he handed his written speech to his fellow Pennsylvanian James Wilson, who read it aloud to the Convention.

Source: Benjamin Franklin, Address to the Federal Convention 1787, Manuscript in the Cornell University Library; found in *An American Primer*, ed. Daniel J. Boorstin, Chicago: University of Chicago Press, 1966, pp. 96-98.

Mr. President,

I confess that I do not entirely approve of this Constitution at present, but Sir, I am not sure I shall never approve it: For having lived long, I have experienced many Instances of being oblig'd, by better Information or fuller Consideration, to change Opinions even on important Subjects, which I once thought right, but found to be otherwise. It is therefore that the older I grow the more apt I am to doubt my own Judgment, and to pay more Respect to the Judgment of others. Most Men indeed as well as most Sects in Religion, think themselves in Possession of all Truth, and that wherever others differ from them it is so far Error. Steele,[4] a Protestant in a Dedication tells the Pope, that the only Difference between our two Churches in their Opinions of the Certainty of their Doctrine, is, the Romish Church is infallible, and the Church of England is never in the Wrong. But tho' many private Persons think almost as highly of their own Infallibility, as of that of their Sect, few express it so naturally as a certain French Lady, who in a little Dispute with her Sister, said, I don't know how it happens, Sister, but I meet with no body but myself that's always in the right. *Il n'y a que moi qui a toujours raison.*[5]

In these Sentiments, Sir, I agree to this Constitution, with all its Faults, if they are such; because I think a General Government necessary for us, and there is no Form of Government but what may be a Blessing to the People if well administred; and I believe farther that this is likely to be well administred for a Course of Years, and can only end in Despotism as other Forms have done before it, when the People shall become so corrupted as to need Despotic Government, being incapable of any other. I doubt too whether any other Convention we can obtain, may be able to make a better Constitution: For when you assemble a Number of Men to have the Advantage of their joint Wisdom, you inevitably assemble with Those Men all their Prejudices, their Passions, their Errors of Opinion, their local Interests, and their selfish Views. From such an Assembly can a perfect

---

[4] Sir Richard Steele (1672-1729) was an Irish-born English playwright, essayist, and journalist.

[5] "There is no one but me who is always right."

Production be expected? It therefore astonishes me, Sir, to find this System approaching so near to Perfection as it does; and I think it will astonish our Enemies, who are waiting with Confidence to hear that our Councils are confounded, like those of the Builders of Babel, and that our States are on the Point of Separation, only to meet hereafter for the Purpose of cutting one anothers Throats. Thus I consent, Sir, to this Constitution because I expect no better, and because I am not sure that it is not the best. The Opinions I have had of its Errors, I sacrifice to the Public Good. I have never whisper'd a Syllable of them abroad. Within these Walls they were born, and here they shall die. If every one of us in returning to our Constituents were to report the Objections he has had to it, and use his Influence to gain Partizans in support of them, we might prevent its being generally received, and thereby lose all the salutary Effects and great Advantages resulting naturally in our favour among foreign Nations, as well as among ourselves, from our real and apparent Unanimity. Much of the Strength and Efficiency of any Government, in procuring and securing Happiness to the People depends on Opinion, on the general Opinion of the Goodness of that Government as well as of the Wisdom and Integrity of its Governors. I hope therefore that for our own Sakes, as a part of the People, and for the sake of our Posterity, we shall act heartily and unanimously in recommending this Constitution, wherever our Influence may extend, and turn our future Thoughts and Endeavours to the Means of having it well administred.

On the whole, Sir, I cannot help expressing a Wish, that every member of the Convention, who may still have Objections to it, would with me on this occasion doubt a little of his own Infallibility, and to make *manifest* our *Unanimity*, put his Name to this instrument.

"A Rising Sun"

Franklin's appeal for unanimity was almost successful. Only three of the delegates in attendance refused to sign the document—Edmund Randolph and George Mason of Virginia, and Elbridge Gerry of Massachusetts. The signing was a moment of triumph, and it was said that Franklin wept as he put his own pen to the document. Madison's notes record a poignant final comment from Franklin.

Source: James Madison, Monday, September 17, 1787, *The Records of the Federal Convention . . ., Op. cit.*

Whilst the last members were signing it Doctr. Franklin looking towards the Presidents Chair, at the back of which a rising sun happened to be painted, observed to a few members near him, that Painters had found it difficult to distinguish in their art a rising from a setting sun. I have, said he, often and often in the course of the Session, and the vicissitudes of my hopes and fears as to its issue, looked at that behind the President without being able to tell whether it was rising or setting: But now at length I have the happiness to know that it is a rising and not a setting Sun.

The Signing of the Constitution, with George Washington presiding (painting by H.C. Christy)

Debate and Ratification

Despite the secrecy rule of the Federal Convention, Franklin's speech quickly found its way into newspapers throughout the United States. (One suspects that the wily old philosopher did not go to great pains to prevent its publication.) Its message of conciliation and compromise proved invaluable during the contentious debate over the Constitution's ratification.

If the issue of America's form of government had seemed dire at the beginning of the Convention, it became even more so once the convention was over. Some critics of the new constitution actually proposed a breakup of the United States into two or three confederacies. Unless ratification was successful, the Union itself might not survive.

Nine States

Now that the Constitution was written, what action was required for it to become the law of the land? The Constitution itself explained this process in a single clear and succinct sentence in Article Seven.

Source: The Constitution of the United States of America, *Great Books of the Western World*, Vol. 43, ed. Robert Maynard Hutchins, Chicago: Encyclopedia Britannica, 1980, pp. 16-17.

The ratification of the Conventions of nine States shall be sufficient for the establishment of this Constitution between the States so ratifying the same.

As we've already noted, the Convention delegates had only been empowered to revise or amend the Articles of Confederations (see Chapter 1). Moreover, their revisions were only to become law upon unanimous agreement by all thirteen states. This was clearly stated in Article Thirteen of the Articles of Confederation.

Source: The Articles of Confederation, *Ibid.*, p. 9.

Article Thirteen

Every State shall abide by the determination of the United States in Congress assembled, on all questions which by this Confederation are submitted to them. And the Articles of this Confederation shall be inviolably observed by every State, and the Union shall be perpetual; nor shall any alteration at any time hereafter be made in any of them, unless such alteration be agreed to in a Congress of the United States, and be afterwards confirmed by the legislatures of every State.

Because the Articles of Confederation were still the law of the land, Article Seven of the proposed Constitution seemed—and indeed, arguably was—illegal. It was, however, remarkably democratic. Instead of turning to the state legislatures for ratification, the Constitution's framers turned to conventions deriving directly from the American people. This reflected a new political idea that the Constitution itself was helping to introduce—that a central government could more effectively reflect the will of the people than could the governments of individual states. (James Wilson, one of the Convention's most active delegates and a tireless proponent of the Constitution during the fight for ratification, described this concept as "federal liberty.")

James Madison himself had argued fervently for reasonably direct ratification as the Federal Convention had neared its end. To him, a constitution not ratified by the people was not a true constitution at all.

Source: James Madison, Monday, July 23, 1787, *The Records of the Federal Convention of 1787*, ed., Max Farrand; in American Memory/Library of Congress, A Century of Lawmaking for a New Nation, 1774-1873, http://lcweb2.loc.gov/ammem/amlaw/lawhome.html.

Mr. (Madison) thought it clear that the Legislatures were incompetent to the proposed changes. These changes would make essential inroads on the State Constitutions, and it would be a novel & dangerous doctrine that a Legislature could change the constitution under which it held its existence.

James Madison
"Father of the Constitution"

There might indeed be some Constitutions within the Union, which had given, a power to the Legislature to concur in alterations of the federal Compact. But there were certainly some which had not; and in the case of these, a ratification must of necessity be obtained from the people. He considered the difference between a system founded on the Legislatures only, and one founded on the people, to be the true difference between a league or treaty, and a Constitution. The former in point of moral obligation might be as inviolable as the latter. In point of political operation, there were two important distinctions in favor of the latter. 1. A law violating a treaty ratified by a preexisting law, might be respected by the Judges as a law, though an unwise or perfidious one.

A law violating a constitution established by the people themselves, would be considered by the Judges as null & void. 2. The doctrine laid down by the law of Nations in the case of treaties is that a breach of any one article by any of the parties, frees the other parties from their engagements. In the case of a union of people under one Constitution, the nature of the pact has always been understood to exclude such an interpretation. Comparing the two modes in point of expediency he thought all the considerations which recommended this Convention in preference to Congress for proposing the reform were in favor of State Conventions in preference to the Legislatures for examining and adopting it.

Doubts about the legality of the Constitution's seventh article were somewhat defused when Congress itself unanimously agreed to submit to the provision. Congress thus set the stage for its own dissolution.

Source: The United States in Congress Assembled, *The Debates of the Several State Conventions on the Adoption of the Federal Constitution*, ed. Jonathan Elite; in American Memory/ Library of Congress, A Century of Lawmaking for a New Nation, 1774-1873, http://lcweb2.loc.gov/ammem/amlaw/lawhome.html.

Friday, September 28, 1787.

Present—New Hampshire, Massachusetts, Connecticut, New York, New Jersey, Pennsylvania, Delaware, Virginia, North Carolina, South Carolina, and Georgia and from Maryland, Mr. Ross.

Congress having received the report of the Convention, lately assembled in Philadelphia, —

Resolved, unanimously, That the said report, with the resolutions and letter accompanying the same, be transmitted to the several legislatures, in order to submit to a convention of delegates, chosen in each state by the people thereof, in conformity to the resolves of the Convention made and provided in that case.

CHARLES THOMPSON, Secretary

George Clinton as "Cato"

Soon after the text of the Constitution was published, the debate over its ratification began in pamphlets and newspapers. New York's governor George Clinton (a future vice president of the United States) wrote numerous articles opposing the Constitution. He used the pen name "Cato," after Cato the Younger, a Roman adversary of Julius Caesar. In the following passage, Clinton argued that the proposed national government would prove inadequate to truly represent the American people.

Source: "Cato" Letter V, *The New-York Journal*, November 22, 1787; in The Constitution Society, http://www.constitution.org/. (Bracketed words are in digital text.)

It is a very important objection to this government, that the representation consists of so few; too few to resist the influence of corruption, and the temptation to treachery, against which all governments ought to take precautions — how guarded you have been on this head, in your own state constitution, and yet the number of senators and representatives proposed for this vast continent, does not equal those of your own state; how great the disparity, if you compare them with the aggregate numbers in the United States. The history of representation in England, from which we have taken our model of legislation, is briefly this: before the institution of legislating by deputies, the whole free part of the community usually met for that purpose; when this became impossible by the increase of numbers the community was divided into districts, from each of which was sent such a number of deputies as was a complete representation of the various numbers and orders of citizens within them; but can it be asserted with truth, that six men can be a complete and full representation of the numbers and various orders of the people in this state? Another thing [that] may be suggested against the small number of representatives is, that but few of you will have the chance of sharing even in this branch of the legislature; and that the choice will be confined to a very few; the more complete it is, the better will your interests be preserved, and the greater the opportunity you will have to participate in government, one of the principal securities of a free people. . . .

The Federalist Papers

Clinton's attacks as "Cato" were highly effective in New York. Alexander Hamilton lashed back in the New York newspapers with some rather impetuous letters signed "Caesar." It was a poor choice of pen names; Julius Caesar was widely regarded during the eighteenth century as the worst of tyrants. Showing more tact, Hamilton went on to publish a letter signed "Publius." Then he enlisted the aid of John Jay and James Madison to help him continue writing letters under this name. Together, Hamilton, Jay, and Madison produced 85 letters which became known as The Federalist Papers. *More than merely a brilliant work of propaganda,* The Federalist Papers *remains a world classic of political philosophy.*

In the first of the Papers, Alexander Hamilton rightly warned that the debate over ratification would become even more heated. He also frankly addressed many people's most worrisome question about the new constitution: Could individual liberties be preserved under a strong central government? Hamilton sternly reminded his readers that liberty was always a trade-off. He also cautioned against manipulative politicians who might prey on their fears.

Source: Alexander Hamilton, Federalist No. 1, *Great Books of the Western World*, Vol. 43, ed. Robert Maynard Hutchins, Chicago: Encyclopedia Britannica, 1980, p. 30.

To judge from the conduct of the opposite parties, we shall be led to conclude that they will mutually hope to evince the justness of their opinions, and to increase the number of their converts by the loudness of their declamations and the bitterness of their invectives. An enlightened zeal for the energy and efficiency of government will be stigmatized as the offspring of a temper fond of despotic power and hostile to the principles of liberty. An over-scrupulous jealousy of danger to the rights of the people, which is more commonly the fault of the head than of the heart, will be represented as mere pretence and artifice, the stale bait for popularity at the expense of the public good. It will be forgotten, on the one hand, that jealousy is the usual concomitant of love, and that the noble enthusiasm of liberty is apt to be infected with a spirit of narrow and illiberal distrust. On the other hand, it will be equally forgotten that the vigour of government is essential to the security of liberty; that, in the contemplation of a sound and well-informed judgment, their interest can never be separated; and that a dangerous ambition more often lurks behind the specious mask of zeal for the rights of the people than under the forbidding appearance of zeal for the firmness and efficiency of government. History will teach us that the former has been found a much more certain road to the introduction of despotism than the latter, and that of those men who have overturned the liberties of republics, the greatest number have begun their career by paying an obsequious court to the people; commencing demagogues, and ending tyrants.

In the second Paper, John Jay made the following eloquent plea for American unity.

Source: John Jay, Federalist No. 2, *Ibid.*, p. 31.

It has often given me pleasure to observe, that independent America was not composed of detached and distant territories, but that one connected, fertile, wide-spreading country was the portion of our western sons of liberty. Providence has in a particular manner blessed it with a variety of soils and productions, and watered it with innumerable streams, for the delight and accommodation of its inhabitants. A succession of navigable waters forms a kind of chain round its borders, as if to bind it together; while the most noble rivers in the world, running at convenient distances, present them with highways for the easy communication of friendly aids, and the mutual transportation and exchange of their various commodities.

With equal pleasure I have as often taken notice, that Providence has been pleased to give this one connected country to one united people—a people descended from the same ancestors, speaking the same language, professing the same religion, attached to the same principles of government, very similar in their manner and customs, and who, by their joint counsels, arms, and efforts, fighting side by side throughout a long and bloody war, have nobly established general liberty and independence.

This country and this people seem to have been made for each other, and it appears as if it was the design of Providence, that an inheritance so proper and convenient for a band of brethren, united to each other by the strongest ties, should never be split into a number of unsocial, jealous, and alien sovereignties.

Similar sentiments have hitherto prevailed among all orders and denominations of men among us. To all general purposes we have uniformly been one people; each individual citizen everywhere enjoying the same national rights, privileges, and protection. As a nation we have made peace and war; as a nation we have vanquished our common enemies; as a nation we have formed alliances, and made treaties, and entered into various compacts and conventions with foreign states.

The Constitution was designed to create a republic, not a direct democracy. In the following passage from the tenth Paper, Madison clarified the difference between the two, arguing the superiority of a former over the latter. He also assured critics that a central, republican government could fairly and justly serve the people of a nation as large as the United States.

Source: James Madison, Federalist No. 10, *Ibid.*, pp. 51-52.

The two great points of difference between a democracy and a republic are: first, the delegation of the government, in the latter, to a small number of citizens elected by the rest; secondly, the greater number of citizens, and greater sphere of country, over which the latter may be extended.

The effect of the first difference is, on the one hand, to refine and enlarge the public views, by passing them through the medium of a chosen body of citizens, whose wisdom may best discern the true interest of their country, and whose patriotism and love of justice will be least likely to sacrifice it to temporary or partial considerations. Under such a regulation, it may well happen that the public voice, pronounced by the representatives of the people, will be more consonant to the public good than if pronounced by the people themselves, convened for the purpose. On the other hand, the effect may be inverted. Men of factious tempers, of local prejudices, or of sinister designs, may, by intrigue, by corruption, or by other means, first obtain the suffrages, and then betray the interests, of the people. The question resulting is, whether small or extensive republics are more favourable to the election of proper guardians of the public weal; and it is clearly decided in favour of the latter by two obvious considerations:

In the first place, it is to be remarked that, however small the republic may be, the representatives must be raised to a certain number, in order to guard against the cabals of a few;

and that, however large it may be, they must be limited to a certain number, in order to guard against the confusion of a multitude. Hence the number of representatives in the two cases not being in proportion to that of the two constituents, and being proportionally greater in the small republic, it follows that, if the proportion of fit characters be not less in the large than in the small republic, the former will present a greater option, and consequently a greater probability of a fit choice.

In the next place, as each representative will be chosen by a greater number of citizens in the large than in the small republic, it will be more difficult for unworthy candidates to practise with success the vicious arts by which elections are too often carried; and the suffrages of the people being more free, will be more likely to centre in men who possess the most attractive merit and the most diffusive and established character.

It must be confessed that in this, as in most other cases, there is a mean, on both sides of which inconveniences will be found to lie. By enlarging too much the number of electors, you render the representative too little acquainted with all their local circumstances and lesser interests; as by reducing it too much, you render him unduly attached to these, and too little fit to comprehend and purpose great and national objects. The federal Constitution forms a happy combination in this respect; the great and aggregate interests being referred to the national, the local and particular to the State legislatures.

The other point of difference is, the greater number of citizens and extent of territory which may be brought within the compass of republican than of democratic government; and it is this circumstance principally which renders factious combinations less to be dreaded in the former than in the latter. The smaller the society, the fewer probably will be the distinct parties and interests composing it; the fewer the distinct parties and interests, the more frequently will a majority be found of the same party; and the smaller the number of individuals composing a majority, and the smaller the compass within which they are placed, the more easily will they concert and execute their plans of oppression. Extend the sphere, and you take in a greater variety of parties and interests; you make it less probable, that a majority of the whole will have a common motive to invade the rights of other citizens; or if such a common motive exists, it will be more difficult for all who feel it to discover their own strength, and to act in unison with each other. Besides other impediments, it may be remarked that, where there is a consciousness of unjust or dishonourable purposes, communication is always checked by distrust in proportion to the number whose concurrence is necessary.

Hence, it clearly appears, that the same advantage which a republic has over a democracy, in controlling the effects of faction, is enjoyed by a large over a small republic—is enjoyed by the Union over the States composing it.

Federalists and Antifederalists

When Hamilton, Jay, Madison, and other supporters of the Constitution referred to themselves as Federalists, they were using the word in a new way. Early during the Federal Convention, delegates who supported state sovereignty were called Federalists, while supporters of a strong central government were called Nationalists. But by the end of the convention, supporters of the Constitution were calling themselves Federalists, and opponents of the Constitution were forced to adopt the more negative label of Antifederalists.

During the debate over ratification, there was still uncertainty over whether the word federal implied a league of loosely-connected states, as it had before the Convention, or a vigorous central government, as it does today. Because of this uncertainty, even an Antifederalist like Richard Henry Lee could write under the pseudonym of the Federal Farmer. In the following passage from his first letter, Lee introduced his principal concern: that the Constitution was intended to create an all-powerful and ultimately tyrannical central government.

Source: Richard Henry Lee, *Letters from the Federal Farmer to the Republican*, Letter I, October 8, 1787; in The Constitution Society, http://www.constitution.org/.

There are three different forms of free government under which the United States may exist as one nation; and now is, perhaps, the time to determine to which we will direct our views.

1. Distinct republics connected under a federal head. In this case the respective state governments must be the principal guardians of the peoples rights, and exclusively regulate their internal police; in them must rest the balance of government. The congress of the states, or federal head, must consist of delegates amenable to, and removable by the respective states: This congress must

have general directing powers; powers to require men and monies of the states; to make treaties; peace and war; to direct the operations of armies, &c. Under this federal modification of government, the powers of congress would be rather advisory or recommendatory than coercive.

2. We may do away the federal state governments, and form or consolidate all the states into one entire government, with one executive, one judiciary, and one legislature, consisting of senators and representatives collected from all parts of the union: In this case there would be a complete consolidation of the states.

3. We may consolidate the states as to certain national objects, and leave them severally distinct independent republics, as to internal police generally. Let the general government consist of an executive, a judiciary, and balanced legislature, and its powers extend exclusively to all foreign concerns, causes arising on the seas to commerce, imports, armies, navies, Indian affairs, peace and war, and to a few internal concerns of the community; to the coin, post offices, weights and measures, a general plan for the militia, to naturalization, and, perhaps to bankruptcies, leaving the internal police of the community, in other respects, exclusively to the state governments; as the administration of justice in all causes arising internally, the laying and collecting of internal taxes, and the forming of the militia according to a general plan prescribed. In this case there would be a complete consolidation, *quo ad*[1] certain objects only.

---

[1] As far as.

Touching the first, or federal plan, I do not think much can be said in its favor: The sovereignty of the nation, without coercive and efficient powers to collect the strength of it, cannot always be depended on to answer the purposes of government; and in a congress of representatives of foreign states, there must necessarily be an unreasonable mixture of powers in the same hands.

As to the second, or complete consolidating plan, it deserves to be carefully considered at this time by every American: If it be impracticable, it is a fatal error to model our governments, directing our views ultimately to it.

The third plan, or partial consolidation, is, in my opinion, the only one that can secure the freedom and happiness of this people. I once had some general ideas that the second plan was practicable, but from long attention, and the proceedings of the convention, I am fully satisfied, that this third plan is the only one we can with safety and propriety proceed upon. Making this the standard to point out, with candor and fairness, the parts of the new constitution which appear to be improper, is my object. The convention appears to have proposed the partial consolidation evidently with a view to collect all powers ultimately, in the United States into one entire government; and from its views in this respect, and from the tenacity of the small states to have an equal vote in the senate, probably originated the greatest defects in the proposed plan.

Violence in Pennsylvania

The debates in the state conventions were often bitter and vindictive, and the votes were perilously close. In Pennsylvania, violence actually broke out over the proposed Constitution.

The Pennsylvania convention voted to ratify, but the Antifederalist minority issued a report protesting a number of serious irregularities. For example, when the Pennsylvania Assembly had been debating whether to hold a ratifying convention, Antifederalist members refused to attend, hoping to deny a quorum for voting on the issue. But a quorum was finally forced by mob violence.

Source: The Address and reasons of dissent of the minority of the convention, of the state of Pennsylvania, to their constituents; Documents from the Continental Congress and the Constitutional Convention, 1774-1789; in Thomas Historical Documents, http://lcweb2.loc.gov/const/ccongquery.html.

The proposed plan had not many hours issued forth from the womb of suspicious secrecy, until such as were prepared for the purpose, were carrying about petitions for people to sign, signifying their approbation of the system, and requesting the legislature to call a convention. While every measure was taken to intimidate the people against opposing it, the public papers teemed with the most violent threats against those who should dare to think for them selves, and *tar and feathers* were liberally promised to all those who would not immediately join in supporting the proposed government be it what it would.—Under each circumstances petitions in favor of calling a convention were signed by great numbers in and about the city, before they had leisure to read and examine the system, many of whom, now they are better acquainted with it, and have had time to investigate its principles, are heartily opposed to it. The petitions were speedily handed in to the legislature.

Affairs were in this situation when on the 28th of September last, a resolution was proposed to the assembly by a member of the house who had been also a member of the federal convention, for calling a state convention, to be elected within ten days for the purpose of examining and adopting the proposed constitution of the United States, though at this time the house had not received it from Congress. This attempt was opposed by a minority, who after offering every argument in their power to prevent the precipitate measure, without effect, absented themselves from the house as the only alternative left them, to prevent the measure taking place previous to their constituents being acquainted with the business—That violence and outrage which had been so often threatened was now practised; some of the members were seized the next day by a mob collected for the purpose, and forcibly dragged to the house, and there detained by force whilst the quorum of the legislature, so formed, compleated their resolution.

Ratification by Virginia

During the Virginia debates, the great orator Patrick Henry took a particularly strong Anti-Federalist stand, raising the familiar argument that the new Constitution would obliterate the rightful power of the states.

Source: Wednesday, June 4, 1788, *The Debates of the Several State Conventions . . ., Op. cit.*

This proposal of altering our federal government is of a most alarming nature! Make the best of this new government—say it is composed by any thing but inspiration—you ought to be extremely cautious, watchful, jealous of your liberty; for, instead of securing your rights, you may lose them forever. If a wrong step be now made, the republic may be lost forever. If this new government will not come up to the expectation of the people, and they shall be disappointed, their liberty will be lost, and tyranny must and will arise. I repeat it again, and I beg gentlemen to consider, that a wrong step, made now, will plunge us into misery, and our republic will be lost. It will be necessary for this Convention to have a faithful historical detail of the facts that preceded the session of the federal Convention, and the reasons that actuated its members in proposing an entire alteration of government, and to demonstrate the dangers that awaited us. If they were of such awful magnitude as to warrant a proposal so extremely perilous as this, I must assert, that this Convention has an absolute right to a thorough discovery of every circumstance relative to this great event. And here I would make this inquiry of those worthy characters who composed a part of the late federal Convention. I am sure they were fully impressed with the necessity of forming a great consolidated government, instead of a confederation. That this is a consolidated government is demonstrably clear; and the danger of such a government is, to my mind, very striking. I have the highest veneration for those gentlemen; but, sir, give me leave to demand, What right had they to say, We, the people? My political curiosity, exclusive of my anxious solicitude for the public welfare, leads me to ask, Who authorized them to speak the language of, We, the people, instead of, We, the states? States are the characteristics and the soul of a confederation. If the states be not the agents of this compact, it must be one great, consolidated, national government, of the people of all the states.

Despite Henry's efforts, the Constitution passed by a narrow vote, making Virginia the ninth state to ratify. With the following words from the Virginia convention, the nation officially adopted the new Constitution.

Source: Wednesday, June 25, 1788, *The Debates of the Several State Conventions . . ., Op. cit.*

We, the delegates of the people of Virginia, duly elected in pursuance of a recommendation from the General Assembly, and now met in Convention, having fully and freely investigated and discussed the proceeding of the federal Convention, and being prepared, as well as the most mature deliberation hath enabled us, to decide thereon, Do, in the name and in behalf of the people of Virginia, declare and make known, that the powers granted under the Constitution, being derived from the people of the United States, be resumed by them whensoever the same shall be perverted to their injury or oppression, and that every power, not granted thereby, remains with them, and at their will; that, therefore, no right, of any denomination, can be cancelled, abridged, restrained, or modified, by the Congress, by the Senate or House of Representatives, acting in any capacity, by the President, or any department or officer of the United States, except in those instances in which power is given by the Constitution for those purposes; and that, among other essential rights, the liberty of conscience and of the press cannot be cancelled, abridged, restrained, or modified, by any authority of the United States.

With these impressions, with a solemn appeal to the Searcher of hearts for the purity of our intentions, and under the conviction that whatsoever imperfections may exist in the Constitution ought rather to be examined in the mode prescribed therein, than to bring the Union into danger by delay, with a hope of obtaining amendments previous to the ratifications,—

We, the said delegates, in the name and behalf of the people of Virginia, do by these presents, assent to and ratify the Constitution, recommended on the seventeenth day of September, one thousand seven hundred and eighty-seven, by the federal Convention, for the government of the United States; hereby announcing to all those whom it may concern, that the said Constitution is binding upon the said people, according to an authentic copy hereto annexed, in the words following.

The Bill of Rights

The ratification of the Constitution was a close call, and the state conventions accepted the document with reservations. The most common objection was the document's lack of a bill of rights. What, critics wondered, was to prevent Congress and a powerful executive from suspending basic human freedoms? Some state conventions proposed amendments to the Constitution to correct this problem.

Jefferson on the Need for a Bill of Rights

Thomas Jefferson was in Paris during the Federal Convention and the ratification process, but he earnestly followed the development of the new Constitution. Although initially a firm believer in the Articles of Confederation, Jefferson was eventually convinced by his friend and protégé James Madison that a new constitution was needed. Upon reading the completed document, Jefferson was favorably impressed—although like many citizens back home, he wanted a bill of rights, as he explained in a letter to Madison.

Source: Thomas Jefferson to James Madison, December 20, 1787; *The Life and Selected Writings of Thomas Jefferson*, ed. Adrienne Koch and William Peden, New York: The Modern Library, 1944, pp. 437-438.

I will now tell you what I do not like. First, the omission of a bill of rights, providing clearly, and without the aid of sophism, for freedom of religion, freedom of the press, protection against standing armies, restriction of monopolies, the eternal and unremitting force of the *habeas corpus* laws,[1] and trials by jury in all matters of fact triable by the laws of

---

[1] *Habeas corpus* is Latin for "having the body." Habeas corpus laws ensure that a person cannot be imprisoned on mere suspicion, nor for a long period without being brought before a court of law.

the land, and not by the laws of nations. To say, as Mr. Wilson[2] does, that a bill of rights was not necessary, because all is reserved in the case of general government which is not given, while in the particular ones, all is given which is not reserved, might do for the audience to which it was addressed; but it is surely a *gratis dictum*,[3] the reverse of which might just as well be said; and it is opposed by strong inferences from the body of the instrument, as well as from the omission of the cause of our present Confederation, which had made the reservation in express terms. It was hard to conclude, because there has been a want of uniformity among the States as to cases triable by jury, because some have been so incautious as to dispense with this mode of trial in certain cases, therefore, the more prudent States shall be reduced to the same level of calamity. It would have been much more just and wise to have concluded the other way, that as most of the States had preserved with jealousy this sacred palladium of liberty, those who had wandered, should be brought back to it; and to have established general right rather than general wrong. For I consider all the ill as established, which may be established. I have a right to nothing, which another has a right to take away; and Congress will have a right to take away trials by jury in all civil cases. Let me add, that a bill of rights is what the people are entitled to against every government on earth, general or particular; and what no just government should refuse, or rest on inference.

---

[2] James Wilson of Pennsylvania was one of the most active delegates at the Federal Convention (see Chapter 2) and a great promoter of the Constitution during the debate over ratification (see Chapter 3).

[3] A statement made voluntarily, and which a person cannot be strictly held to.

Hamilton's Opposition to a Bill of Rights

Under the new Federal Government, Alexander Hamilton would become one of Jefferson's fiercest adversaries. So it is hardly surprising that the two men took opposite views concerning the need for a bill of rights. In Federalist 84, Alexander Hamilton argued that such amendments would be a dangerous redundancy.

Source: Alexander Hamilton, Federalist No. 84, *Great Books of the Western World*, Vol. 43, ed. Robert Maynard Hutchins, Chicago: Encyclopedia Britannica, 1980, pp. 253.

The truth is, after all the declamations we have heard, that the Constitution is itself, in every rational sense, and to every useful purpose, A BILL OF RIGHTS. The several bills of rights in Great Britain form its Constitution, and conversely the constitution of each State is its bill of rights. And the proposed Constitution, if adopted, will be the bill of rights of the Union. Is it one object of a bill of rights to declare and specify the political privileges of the citizens in the structure and administration of the government? This is done in the most ample and precise manner in the plan of the convention; comprehending various precautions for the public security, which are not to be found in any of the State constitutions. Is another object of a bill of rights to define certain immunities and modes of proceeding, which are relative to personal and private concerns? This we have seen has also been attended to, in a variety of cases, in the same plan. Adverting therefore to the substantial meaning of a bill of rights, it is absurd to allege that it is not to be found in the work of the convention. It may be said that it does not go far enough, though it will not be easy to make this appear; but it can with no propriety be contended that there is no such thing.

The Magna Carta

A legal guarantee of rights was far from a uniquely American idea, much less a new one. The first English bill of rights dates back to 1215 A.D. In that year, the English barons forced King John to sign the Magna Carta, or "great charter." This was the first British document to seriously limit the absolute power of kings. In the following two items (translated from the Latin original), the Magna Carta touched on the rights of the accused.

Source: The Magna Carta; in United Kingdom Legal Information Centre, http://wwlia.org/uk-home.htm.

- In future no official shall place a man on trial upon his own unsupported statement, without producing credible witnesses to the truth of it.

- No free man shall be seized or imprisoned, or stripped of his rights or possessions, or outlawed or exiled, or deprived of his standing in any other way, nor will we proceed with force against him, or send others to do so, except by the lawful judgement of his equals or by the law of the land.

The Magna Carta even went so far as to hint that rebellion was justified if a king refused to recognize the rights of his subjects. (The "us" in the following item refers to the king.)

Source: *Ibid.*

- Any man who so desires may take an oath to obey the commands of the twenty-five barons for the achievement of these ends, and to join with them in assailing us to the utmost of his power. We give public and free permission to take this oath to any man who so desires, and at no time will we prohibit any man from taking it. Indeed, we will compel any of our subjects who are unwilling to take it to swear it at our command.

- That the raising or keeping a standing army within the kingdom in time of peace, unless it be with consent of parliament, is against law.
- That the subjects which are protestants, may have arms for their defence suitable to their conditions, and as allowed by law.
- That election of members of parliament ought to be free.
- That the freedom of speech, and debates or proceedings in parliament, ought not to be impeached or questioned in any court or place out of parliament.
- That excessive bail ought not to be required, nor excessive fines imposed; nor cruel and unusual punishments inflicted.
- That jurors ought to be duly impanelled and returned, and jurors which pass upon men in trials of high treason ought to be freeholders.[4]
- That all grants and promises of fines and forfeitures of particular persons before conviction, are illegal and void.
- And that for redress of all grievances, and for the amending, strengthening and preserving of the laws, parliaments ought to be held frequently.

---

[4] Landowners.

The English Bill of Rights

In the late seventeenth century, the "divine right of kings" was further eroded by the Glorious Revolution, which made William of Orange and his wife, Mary, king and queen of England. In 1689, William and Mary agreed to the English Bill of Rights, which included the following items.

Source: The English Bill of Rights; in *Ibid.*

And thereupon the said lords spiritual and temporal, and commons, pursuant to their respective letters and elections, being now assembled in a full and free representative of this nation, taking into their most serious consideration the best means for attaining the ends aforesaid; do in the first place (as their ancestors in like cases have usually done) for the vindicating and asserting their ancient rights and liberties, declare:

- That the pretended power of suspending of laws, or the execution of laws, by regal authority, without consent of parliament, is illegal.
- That the pretended power of dispensing with laws, or the executions of laws, by regal authority, as it hath been assumed and exercised of late, is illegal.
- That the commission for erecting the late court of commissioners for ecclesiastical causes, and all other commissions and courts of like nature are illegal and pernicious.
- That levying money for or to the use of the crown, by pretence of prerogative, without grant of parliament, for longer time, or in other manner than the same is or shall be granted, is illegal.
- That it is the right of the subjects to petition the King, and all commitments and prosecutions for such petitioning are illegal.

The Virginia Bill of Rights

The delegates at the Federal Convention considered themselves heirs to this English tradition of fundamental rights. They did not include an actual bill of rights in the Constitution because most of them believed (as Hamilton argued in Federalist 84) that the document essentially was a bill of rights.

George Mason of Virginia strongly disagreed with this viewpoint and made a failed, last-minute effort to include a bill of rights in the Constitution. Mason had already distinguished himself in this area, having drafted a bill of rights for Virginia in 1776. (Several other states also included bills of rights in their constitutions.)

Adopted on June 12, 1776, the Virginia Declaration of Rights is printed in its entirety below. It influenced the writing of the Declaration of Independence of 1776 as well as the United States Bill of Rights of 1791. Note how some of Mason's ideas can be traced to the English Bill of Rights—and even to the Magna Carta.

Source: The Virginia Declaration of Rights; in Statutes at Large of Virginia, ed. W. W. Hening, 1821; also in *Sources and Documents Illustrating the American Revolution and the Formation of the Federal Constitution, 1764-1788*, ed. S. E. Morrison, London: Oxford University Press, 1923.

AT A GENERAL CONVENTION of Delegates and Representatives, from the several counties and corporations of Virginia, held at the Capitol in the City of Williamsburg on Monday the 6th May 1776.

A declaration of Rights made by the representatives of the good people of Virginia, assembled in full and free Convention; which rights do pertain to them and their posterity, as the basis and foundation of government.

1. That all men are by nature equally free and independent, and have certain inherent rights, of which, when they enter into a state of society, they cannot by any compact deprive or divest their posterity; namely, the enjoyment of life and liberty, with the means of acquiring and possessing property, and pursuing and obtaining happiness and safety.

2. That all power is vested in, and consequently derived from, the people; that magistrates are their trustees and servants, and at all times amenable to them.

3. That government is, or ought to be instituted for the common benefit, protection, and security of the people, nation, or community; of all the various modes and forms of government, that is best which is capable of producing the greatest degree of happiness and safety, and is most effectually secured against the danger of maladministration; and that when any government shall be found inadequate or contrary to these purposes, a majority of the community hath an indubitable, unalienable and indefeasible right to reform, alter or abolish it, in such manner as shall be judged most conducive to the public weal.

4. That no man, or set of men, are entitled to exclusive or separate emoluments or privileges from the community, but in consideration of publick services; which, not being descendible, neither ought the offices of magistrate, legislator or judge to be hereditary.

5. That the legislative and executive powers of the state should be separate and distinct from the judiciary; and that the members of the two first may be restrained from oppression, by feeling and participating the burthens of the people, they should, at fixed periods, be reduced to a private station, return into that body from which they were originally taken, and the vacancies be supplied by frequent, certain, and regular elections, in which all, or any part of the former members to be again eligible or ineligible, as the laws shall direct.

6. That elections of members to serve as representatives of the people in assembly, ought to be free; and that all men having sufficient evidence of permanent common

interest with, and attachment to the community, have the right of suffrage, and cannot be taxed or deprived of their property for publick uses, without their own consent, or that of their representatives so elected, not bound by any law to which they have not, in like manner, assented for the public good.

7. That all power of suspending laws, or the executive of laws, by any authority without consent of the representatives of the people, is injurious to their rights, and ought not to be exercised.

8. That in all capital or criminal prosecutions a man hath a right to demand the cause and nature of his accusation, to be confronted with the accusers and witnesses, to call for evidence in his favour, and to a speedy trial by an impartial jury of his vicinage, without whose unanimous consent he cannot be found guilty; nor can he be compelled to give evidence against himself; that no man be deprived of his liberty, except by the law of the land or the judgment of his peers.

9. That excessive bail ought not to be required, nor excessive fines imposed, nor cruel and unusual punishments inflicted.

10. That general warrants, whereby an officer or messenger may be commanded to search suspected places without evidence of a fact committed, or to seize any person or persons not named, or whose offence is not particularly described and supported by evidence, are grievous and oppressive, and ought not to be granted.

11. That in controversies respecting property, and in suits between man and man, the ancient trial by jury is preferable to any other, and ought to be held sacred.

12. That the freedom of the press is one of the great bulwarks of liberty, and can never be restrained but by despotick governments.

13. That a well-regulated militia, composed of the body of the people trained to arms, is the proper, natural and safe defence of a free state; that standing armies in time of peace should be avoided as dangerous to liberty; and that in all cases the military should be under strict subordination to, and governed by, the civil power.

14. That the people have a right to uniform government; and, therefore, that no government separate from, or independent of the government of Virginia, ought to be erected or established within the limits thereof.

15. That no free government, or the blessings of liberty, can be preserved to any people, but by a firm adherence to justice, moderation, temperance, frugality and virtue, and by frequent recurrence to fundamental principles.

16. That religion, or the duty which we owe to our Creator, and the manner of discharging it, can be directed only by reason and conviction, not by force or violence; and therefore all men are equally entitled to the free exercise of religion, according to the dictates of conscience; and that it is the mutual duty of all to practise Christian forbearance, love, and charity towards each other.

The U.S. Bill of Rights

When the new Constitution went into effect on March 4, 1789, skeptics wondered if the new government would comply with the state conventions' earlier demands for amendments. But James Madison, now a member of the House of Representatives, sponsored a series of amendments in July. In September, Congress used these as the basis of twelve proposed amendments. The first two were eventually discarded, while the remaining ten were adopted as the United States Bill of Rights on December 15, 1791.

Source: The Bill of Rights, *Great Books . . ., Op. cit.*

Article One

Congress shall make no law respecting an establishment of religion, or prohibiting the free exercise thereof; or abridging the freedom of speech, or of the press; or the right of the people peaceably to assemble, and to petition the Government for a redress of grievances.

Article Two

A well-regulated militia being necessary to the security of a free State, the right of the people to keep and bear arms shall not be infringed.

Article Three

No soldier shall, in time of peace, be quartered in any house, without the consent of the owner, nor in time of war but in a manner to be prescribed by law.

Article Four

The right of the people to be secure in their persons, houses, papers, and effects, against unreasonable searches and seizures, shall not be violated, and no warrants shall issue, but upon probable cause, supported by oath or affirmation, and particularly describing the place to be searched, and the persons or things to be seized.

Article Five

No person shall be held to answer for a capital, or otherwise infamous crime, unless on a presentment or indictment of a Grand Jury, except in cases arising in the land or naval forces, or in the militia, when in actual service in time of war or public danger; nor shall any person be subject for the same offense to be twice put in jeopardy of life or limb; nor shall be compelled in any criminal case to be a witness against himself, nor be deprived of life, liberty, or property, without due process of law; nor shall private property be taken for public use, without just compensation.

Article Six

In all criminal prosecutions the accused shall enjoy the right to a speedy and public trial, by an impartial jury of the State and district wherein the crime shall have been committed, which district shall have been previously ascertained by law, and to be informed of the nature and cause of the accusation; to be confronted with the witnesses against him; to have compulsory process for obtaining witnesses in his favor, and to have the assistance of counsel for his defense.

Article Seven

In suits at common law, where the value of controversy shall exceed twenty dollars, the right of trial by jury shall be preserved, and no fact tried by a jury shall be otherwise re-examined in any court of the United States, than according to the rules of the common law.

Article Eight

Excessive bail shall not be required, nor excessive fines imposed, nor cruel and unusual punishments inflicted.

Article Nine

The enumeration of the Constitution of certain rights shall not be construed to deny or disparage others retained by the people.

Article Ten

The powers not delegated to the United States by the Constitution, nor prohibited by it to the States, are reserved to the States respectively or to the people.

Epilogue:
A Rebel Dies, a Charter Endures
by Wim Coleman

Daniel Shays died on September 29, 1825, in Sparta, New York. In his last years, he had been granted a pension for his courageous service in the Revolutionary War, which included the Battle of Bunker Hill. At the time of his death, Shays was no longer feared as a dangerous rebel. Thanks to the U.S. Constitution and its Bill of Rights, the nation seemed more secure than it had when Shays made his desperate attack on Springfield in 1786—secure enough to treat an old rebel with honor and generosity.

The United States Constitution is the oldest written national constitution in the world. It and the Bill of Rights have weathered many storms of state, including the Civil War, the Great Depression, the impeachments of two presidents, and the resignation in disgrace of another. What is the secret of the success and longevity of these founding documents?

For one thing, the framers in Philadelphia knew what they were doing. Anything but the starry-eyed idealists sometimes portrayed in schoolbooks, they were tough-minded and even self-interested men of business and politics. They knew their history and understood the needs of their new nation. They used their considerable knowledge to create a document that would last, despite staggering changes that they could not possibly anticipate.

One of their masterstrokes was a beautifully designed system of checks and balances, inspired by the theories of the French political philosopher Montesquieu. The legislative, executive, and judicial branches of the U.S. government work intricately together, and yet their powers are carefully separated so that no single branch can ever seize absolute power. While many governments throughout the world have succumbed to totalitarian control during the last two centuries, the United States has been spared this misfortune, largely because of our government's separation of powers.

The framers also made brilliant use of language that was at once lucidly plain and cunningly ambiguous. Because of its ambiguity, the Constitution could be endlessly reinterpreted to fit the ever-changing facts of American life.

Consider, for example, the Constitution's opening words: "We, the people of the United States . . ." Crafted by that masterful prose stylist Gouverneur Morris partly to avoid a tedious and unwieldy list of states, this elegant phrase has changed greatly in meaning. To Morris and his contemporaries, "the people" constituted a rather elite group—free, white, male property owners, at the exclusion of everyone else. Little by little, the phrase has become more and more inclusive as rights have been extended to African Americans, women, and people who do not own land. Morris could hardly have imagined how we read his language today.

This sort of ambiguity helps create an endlessly revitalizing tension between liberty and constraint. Together, the Constitution and Bill of Rights are neither authoritarian nor purely democratic; by constant reinterpretation, they cover an ever-shifting middle ground. These two documents are, in fact, wonderfully complementary—the Constitution explaining what government must do, the Bill of Rights explaining what government must not do. After eight years as America's first president, George Washington spoke eloquently of this seemingly miraculous tension in his Farewell Address.

Source: George Washington, Farewell Address; found in *An American Primer*, ed. Daniel J. Boorstin, Chicago: University of Chicago Press, 1966, p. 218.

This Government, the offspring of your own choice, uninfluenced and unawed, adopted upon full investigation and mature deliberation, completely free in its principles, in the distribution of its powers, uniting security with energy, and containing within itself a provision for its own amendment, has a just claim to your confidence and your support. Respect for its authority, compliance with its laws, acquiescence in its measures, are duties enjoined by the fundamental maxims of true liberty. The basis of our political systems is the right of the people to make and to alter their constitutions of government. But the constitution which at any time exists till changed by an explicit and authentic act of the whole people is sacredly obligatory upon all.

George Washington

Bibliography

Books:

Boorstin, Daniel J., ed. *An American Primer.* Chicago: University of Chicago Press, 1966.

Bowen, Catherine Drinker. *Miracle at Philadelphia: The Story of the Constitutional Convention May to September 1787.* Boston: Atlantic-Little, Brown, 1966.

Coleman, Wim, ed. *The Declaration of Independence.* Carlisle, MA: Discovery Enterprises, Ltd., 1997.

Hutchins, Robert Maynard, ed. *Great Books of the Western World,* Vol. 43 (American State Papers, The Federalist, J. S. Mill). Encyclopedia Britannica, 1980.

Koch, Adrienne and William Peden, eds. *The Life and Selected Writings of Thomas Jefferson.* New York: The Modern Library, 1944.

Latham, Earl, ed. *The Declaration of Independence and the Constitution* (3rd edition). Massachusetts: D. C. Heath, 1976.

Morrison, S. E., ed. *Sources and Documents Illustrating the American Revolution and the Formation of the Federal Constitution, 1764-1788.* London: Oxford University Press, 1923.

Websites:

American Memory/Library of Congress, A Century of Lawmaking for a New Nation, 1774-1873, http://lcweb2.loc.gov/ammem/amlaw/lawhome.html

American Memory/Library of Congress, George Washington Papers at the Library of Congress, 1741-1799, http://memory.loc.gov/ammem/gwhtml/gwhome.html

The Constitution Society, http://www.constitution.org/

Longman's American History Online, http://longman.awl.com/history/home.htm

Thomas Historical Documents, http://lcweb2.loc.gov/const/ccongquery.html

United Kingdom Legal Information Centre, http://wwlia.org/uk-home.htm

The University of Oklahoma Law Center, A Chronology of U.S. Historical Documents, http://www.law.ou.edu/hist/